How to play the Didjeridoo:
A practical guide for everyone

Jonathan Cope

with thanks and respect to the
Australian Aboriginal people

First published in 2000 by Wild Wind.
E-mail to

A catalogue record for this book is available from the British
Library.

ISBN 0-9539811-0-X

Illustrations, design, and layout by Jonathan Cope.

CONTENTS

INTRODUCTION

This book is for anyone interested in learning to play the didjeridoo (hereafter shortened to 'didj'). If you want to cut-to-the-chase and dive straight into the learning to play section please go to page 18. Those wishing to know a little more about the background of the instrument and Aboriginal culture, and this text is by no means an exhaustive survey, please read on. Whatever your level of interest in the didjeridoo I would point out that to use the didj, without knowing a little of its background, seems a little disrespectful (in my opinion).

A section on FAQs (Frequently Asked Questions – terrible computer jargon, sorry) is followed by an overview of what makes a 'good' didj and selecting, or making, one suitable for you. After this I go straight into an in-depth guide to getting to grips with the intricacy of playing this wonderful instrument. There are sections that deal with more advanced techniques and exercises, along with a practical how-to for making wax mouthpieces, and even didjeridoos and bags to carry them in. A later section gives a brief list of places to buy didjs, associated items, CDs, tapes, books, supplies, and some didj-related Internet web-site addresses. Lastly, if you are particularly interested, you will find some information about the author.

FAQ's

What is a didjeridoo?

The Australian Aboriginal culture, whom we must thank for sharing this great instrument with us, is thought to be in excess of 100,000 years old and it is quite possible that the didj is the oldest woodwind instrument known. In practical terms, a 'didj' can be any tube of material that can be made to resonate by air passing down it when a person plays it. It is possible to use many types of material to make didjs: plastic, bamboo, metal, ceramic, etc. All have their good and bad points. Traditionally, didjs are made from one of several types of eucalyptus wood, though it is probable that the 'Yolngu' or Aboriginal people may have first played didjs made from bamboo, which grows wild in much of Northern Australia.

How are didjs made?

I'll cover the manufacture of 'alternative' didjs later on. What follows is a brief explanation of traditional didj construction.

Eucalyptus trees grow in abundance all year round in the tropical scrublands of Northern Australia and there are several species of tree: Bloodwood, Red Stringybark and Woolly Butt, to name the main ones. Termites, or white ants, lay their eggs at the base of the tree and the hatching larvae eat into and up inside the centre of the tree, hollowing it out. The didj maker comes along, tapping on the trees with a stone until the hollow ones are found. He then cuts down the chosen tree, trims the hollow section to a suitable length (anything from 60 – 180 cms long), washes out any debris (including ants!!), strips off the outer bark and roughly shapes the didj. With the massive increase in demand for 'euc' didjs caused by the growing popularity of the instrument outside Australia, the Aboriginal people are working hard to ensure that the removal of trees is done carefully and thoughtfully so as not to disturb the eco-system too greatly. Having cut and seasoned the wood, the experienced maker will then take note of the various features such as the length, girth and bore of the wood. These features will be used to shape the wood and arrive at a didj that is 'keyed' to a certain pitch before final decoration, varnishing or painting, and finishing off with a bees-wax mouthpiece.

What are didjs used for?

Traditionally didjs are used in secret and non-secret ceremonies, rituals and initiation rites, and to celebrate the Australian Aborigine's rich spiritual beliefs. Didjs are often painted with designs that reflect the characters found in the stories of Aboriginal 'Dreamtime', a complex creation 'myth' that I couldn't begin to do justice to here (check out the bibliography section for more info). Animals feature in a lot of paintings, they signify the adopted totem animal that each Aboriginal child is thought to have descended from, such as a kangaroo or a bush wallaby. Often the individual tribe's secret ceremonies give way to gatherings that are inter-tribal, these are known as corroborees. Whether a secret ceremony or a corroboree, there are a select group of people involved in the re-enactment of a Dreamtime story. Usually a trio consisting of a Songman, who sets the rhythm with 'bilma' or clapsticks and sings the main part of a song, a didj player, and a dancer perform the main elements of the story with other people joining in. Songs can be short or last for days(!) and are passed down the generations to carefully chosen Elders or 'clevermen' as many of the elements are considered very secret. Additional instruments such as 'Tjuringu' or bullroarers (an oval, wing-sectioned, piece of wood that is spun around the head on a cord, producing a whirring noise thought to ward off evil) and boomerangs slapped together, are used to further embellish the song.

To a growing number of non-aboriginal folk the didj can be used for many things. In our often crazy world full of stresses and distractions, more folk are turning to all things 'alternative' whilst looking for a way to wind down or stay sane! The didj is becoming increasingly popular in various forms of anti-stress therapy and has become synonymous with the desire to feel more in touch with our ancient tribal 'roots' – wherever we are from.

Listening to, or even better playing, didj is a great aid for relaxation - its deeply rooted primal drone and the medatitive breathing techniques used when playing can really help calm the mind, body and spirit.

Didjs may also find use in work with those with mental problems, so-called 'difficult-learners', and in 'sound massage', where a didj is played over a person's body to allow the sound vibrations and subtle harmonics to ease away troubles. Perhaps the single most popular use for the complex sounds of the didj, outside traditional playing, is for accompaniment to more 'western' styles of music - anything from Acid Jazz to Folk or Progressive Rock. The didjeridoo is an excellent woodwind instrument that is easily played by anyone who cares to learn, without need for highly technical knowledge of music, and is capable of extreme diversity in the range of sounds that can be produced.

Where do didjs come from?

The didjeridoo originates from certain parts of Australia, mainly the central Northern Territories, i.e. Arnhemland. This is due in part to the availability of the raw materials of eucalyptus trees (and termites!), rather than any cultural difference between different regional tribes. Didjs are now found and played over most of Australia by many Aboriginal players (along with a growing throng of non-aboriginal folk!).

Where did the name come from?

The term didjeridoo (and there are lots of variations: didgeridoo, didjeridu, etc.) is purely a western invention thought to represent the sound as heard by the early non-aboriginal explorers - the rhythmic playing of the didj in a more traditional way often produces this kind of sound pattern. The Aboriginal peoples have different regional names for the didj. From the more popular 'Yidaki' (which means 'sound-stick' and is used by the Yolngu people of several tribes in Central Arnhemland) to 'Gunbaark' and 'Yurlunggur'.

Selecting a didj

Didjs can be made from a wide variety of materials but there are several factors involved in the choosing or making of one: ethics, cost, personal preference, practicality and sound quality. I would not fault the view that, in the ideal world, everyone wishing to play a didj should purchase a eucalyptus didj made by a Yolngu maker (working alone or within the environment of a recognised workers co-operative) from an ethically-minded dealer or distributor. However, instruments of this type entail a good deal of skilled work and, by the time they have had all the various costs involved in getting them into a shop near you added, are pretty expensive. Although relatively speaking, when compared to many other instruments, a Euc didj represents very good value for money you should expect to pay in excess of UK£200, this price may be higher or even double for some European countries. This is especially true for a didj that has come from a recognised maker and as is not a product of the increasingly popular tourist market.

There are many people supplying the growing demand for didjs via cheaper alternatives from other countries such as India and Indonesia. I am not saying this is wrong, although anyone selling a didj of this type as the 'real thing' from Australia's Yolngu people deserves to get termites in their pants. However, it does seem a shame to see the money a didj sale produces not going back to the people who originated this instrument. I guess this ideal has to find balance with the demand for the instrument, the desire to try other materials and styles, and to provide a wide range of pricing bands. I don't wish to try and cover ethical questions such as this, along with the very thorny political and humane issues surrounding the Yolngu (Aboriginal) peoples of Australia in a publication of this type. I will leave this to more in-depth publications and suggest you check the book listings for more info.

Different types of didj

At the 'lower' end of the scale, didjs can be made from lengths of plastic pipe. Any plastic, or at a pinch metal, pipe about 100+ cms in length with a bore of about 3-5cms can perform as a fine 'starter' didj. The low cost of extruded plastic plumbing pipe from a DIY store means it is possible to put together a didj of this type for a few pounds. All you need do is file off the cut ends to leave a smooth finish and add some beeswax – see p.38. If you are really pushed you can even use a cardboard tube of similar dimensions. As with all types of didj the mouthpiece should be not too large or too small – try it out for size before you buy if you can (this has led to some humorous moments in large DIY stores!). Plastic didjs don't need much on-going attention and you can even wash them out if you need to.

Different types of didjeridoos

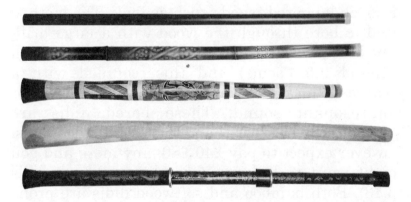

From top:
plastic pipe, bamboo, bored out soft-wood, termite-bored eucalyptus, Slidedidge.

In the mid-range come didjs made from bamboo or softwood that have been drilled through. Bamboo didjs can come from Australia and may have had some Aboriginal involvement in their production but they are more likely to be from Indonesia and be made by someone who has never played a didj. Expect to pay about £20-£40. These didjs are light and often feature a burnt decoration using elements from Aboriginal designs and, although they certainly sound better than most 'pipe' didjs, they can be fragile.

Softwood, and occasionally hardwood, bored didjs are becoming increasingly better in terms of quality, finish and sound but there are still some traps for the unwary. Be aware that didjs of this type are often from countries where unregulated deforestation can mean that the didj may be made from 'endangered' woods such as teak. The method used to bore through the wood with a large drill-type bit can mean that the bore may be quite small (around 2.5-3.5cms) and this, coupled with a relatively thick didj wall, can lead to a muffled or non-resonant sound. These bored didjs are substantially cheaper than other 'solid' wood didjs, however expect to pay £40-£80; any more and you might want to look out for split-wood type didjs (p.13). Both bamboo and softwood didjs are prone to damage by temperature and humidity so protect them from extremes and from excessive moisture, as they can split or rot.

At the higher end of the didj spectrum come split-wood didjs and, of course, the termite hollowed eucalyptus type. Split didjs are made from many different kinds of wood; ash, chestnut, oak and yew to name a few. As the name implies, didjs of this kind are made by splitting a suitable section of wind-fallen timber in half, hollowing out the middle of each half and then gluing the two halves back together. This can be fraught with difficulties and should not be undertaken lightly – it helps to have some basic wood-working experience. Those interested to know more and have the necessary bravery and skill can check out p. 41-45.

Although some people would argue that a split-wood didj can never have all the subtlety of a termite-hollowed didj I would say that there are some superbly skilled makers out there. In the right hands it is possible to produce an instrument of extremely high sound quality for around half the price of a eucalyptus didj. Expect to pay £90-£180. My personal favourite of the didjs I own (and my girlfriend tells me I have far too many! from euc to plastic pipe) is a beautiful piece of English sycamore that has been fashioned into a very powerful didj in the key of D by Ant Scott at Antic Earthworks. (Cheers Ant!). Split didjs should only really use seasoned wood, if not they may be prone to splitting along the join. If you spot this early enough you may be able to stop it spreading with some carefully applied specialist wood glue. Protect from extremes of temperature and avoid knocks.

Of course the ultimate goal for anyone who plans to really feel 'connected' to their didj, and its origins, is to own a termite-bored eucalyptus. Being a very hard and dense wood euc has a life of its own when it comes to coaxing the infinite spectrum of subtle harmonics from those termite grooves! Purchase of a euc didj made in Australia will all but guarantee to make you feel good (more like a 'real' didj player?). It will also give you the satisfaction that at least part of your money is finding it's way into the communities that breathed life into this instrument in the first place. However, there are still factors to be aware of when choosing a euc:

Take a good look at it the didj, is it reasonably straight or does it have real kinks and curves in it? being natural they will never be completely straight but avoid any that are really 'curly'. Pick up the didj and mentally weigh it up against its size, bearing in mind that eucalyptus is a very dense wood. Look down the didj, or preferably 'up' it, can you see light easily? This might be difficult if it has much of a curve in it but what you are looking to judge is the thickness of the walls, avoid any that have walls much thicker than 1.5cms and have obvious blockages or obstructions. When playing, the whole length of the didj will resonate to create that wonderfully rich sound and any thick bits or obstructions will hamper this. Although it is possible to 'tune' a didj, by cutting its length down or boring out either end, I would not recommend it with decorated didjs and it is certainly not a practice for the faint-hearted!

Check the mouthpiece for size against your face, if it has not been finished off you can of course alter the size with beeswax. Remember that you can reduce the interior diameter of the mouthpiece with wax but it is very hard to enlarge the actual wood, if the mouthpiece has wax already then you will be able to mould it to fit. Try blowing down the didj, what does it sound like? If you are a beginner you might invite a more seasoned friend along to really give the didj a test-drive. Some players slap the playing end of the didj with the flat of their hand to access the sound characteristics, i.e. the amount of resonance and the sustain or delay in the sound dying away. If the sound dies pretty quickly then it may be difficult to attain a really advanced drone sound, too much sustain and it may sound like the over modulated sound you get from most plastic pipes.

Check the didj all over, and particularly at either end, for cracks, splits or holes. Although small cracks and holes can be repaired with beeswax or modern fillers, too much damage can affect the sound and may lead to the didj literally vibrating itself to bits! Try to seal the large end of the didj onto a carpeted floor and blow down the playing end listening for any wheezing or whistling as air escapes from holes. Any loss of pressure when playing will seriously affect your ability to drone. Happy with the didj of your choice? OK, then buy it and carry your purchase proudly home, where you can reap the benefits of your sound choice.

Eucalyptus didjs are usually more resilient than other wood didjs as they are made from seasoned hard wood, even so you should still treat them with respect and follow the guidelines for the split type mentioned previously. Hopefully you will care enough for your didj that you will treat it to a nice, preferably padded, carry bag to protect it. If you are a whizz with a sewing machine you can make your own (see p.46). This goes for all didjs, a carry bag will far out-weigh its cost in terms of protection for your instrument.

Ultimately you must choose the didj that is right for you. If you are a beginner you might want to get something that is of medium length (say 130cms) and has a relatively small bore (3-5cms) with a mouthpiece around 3.5cms in internal diameter. These dimensions will enable you to drone more readily and get the most from a lungful of air, as you become more proficient you will find you can play didjs of any size, but until then large didjs can take large amounts of air. If physics meant much in the world of didjeridoos then short didjs should be higher pitched and longer ones lower pitched but look out for the contradictions!

Specials: a few types of didj that don't easily fit into the classifications above! As didjs gain in popularity more and more inventive people are trying all kinds of crazy, and not so crazy, things with the format of the basic didj. Closely fitting sections of pipe, usually plastic, with suitable seals can allow a didj player to slide the fundamental note like a slide trombone. These slide didjs are finding favour with players who play alongside other musicians as they allow the didj to be tuned to match just about any pitched instrument for harmony in accompaniment. A very good slide didj is made by Scott Dunbarr of Slidedidge in Australia – this three-piece slide has the range of almost a full octave and is great for travelling with.

I have also seen didjs made from extruded and fired clay, if they have a spiral shape they can be compact and often end up pointing back at the player; good for hearing what you sound like. However, they are very fragile and are often expensive so have limited appeal. Occasionally someone alters an existing instrument to be played more like a didj; amongst the more successful of the conversions I've seen was a Tibetan trumpet with its top few inches removed to give a wider playing aperture and it sounded pretty good (Wills you know who you are!).

A quick search on the internet, as well as being a great way to find a lot of wonderful information about didjs, will quickly reveal all manner of wild experiments into differing didj formats.

Playing: 1). The basic drone.

OK, hopefully you felt it was important to know more about where didjs come from and are now bursting to try for yourself. If you have dashed straight to this section then let your enthusiasm take you further but pop back and read the earlier stuff whilst you take a break from playing later on.

It may seem unnecessary but I'm going to suggest that you take a minute or two to 'warm up' the various bits of yourself that will be used in playing, i.e. your lips, cheeks, lungs and diaphragm. If you're anything like me when I first got my hands on a didj I was so eager I tried and tried for hours and ended up with a fat lip – so take it easy! Take yourself and your didj off somewhere comfortable where there will not be too many distractions. Whilst sitting, take some nice, slow, deep breaths – maybe exaggerating some of the out-breaths by 'puffing' your cheeks and really blowing out. The aim is not to hyper-ventilate and end up dizzy, just to get your lungs ready for some use. Next breathe out forcefully, through a closed mouth, so that your lips have no alternative other than to vibrate. Aim to breathe out pretty slowly so they really flap about and you end up doing a child's horse impression. (If you are getting self-conscious you better worry 'cos it gets a lot crazier soon!).

Once you are happy with your 'horse' try doing this down the didj – just place your lips in the (hopefully) bees-waxed end of the didj and blow. There is divided opinion on whether playing 'face-on', with the didj in the centre of your lips, or off to the left or right is the 'right' way. I started off playing to one side and still change from that way to 'face-on' depending on what style of playing I'm aiming for – just try each way and see what suits you. Back to the didj, the idea is that you pout your lips slightly whilst they are in the didj, with the bottom lip sticking out just a bit further than the top, and do your horse impression again. Aim to have the mouthpiece on the centre of your mouth vertically, not touching your nose or your chin, unless the didj is very thick at the playing end.

Hopefully a wonderful drone should emerge from the other end of the didj; and you might want to play into a corner so that the sound bounces back and you can hear it. If you make a spluttering noise, a 'trumpet' tone or it sounds more like a fart down a drainpipe don't worry, my first efforts were worse, believe me. The trick is not to try too hard, if you have ever playing a woodwind instrument before I'm going to suggest that you might be at a disadvantage as you will probably be using a tight-lipped 'embouchure'. If you don't know what that means then you're *probably* going to find this easier.

Don't blow too hard, leave your mouth pressed comfortably against the mouth-piece – too hard and you will end up with tooth ache, too loose and air will leak out the sides, where you join the didj. If the drone sounds a bit weak or airy try to get a good seal and keep your lips loose and wet. Experiment by making your lips looser or tighter than they currently are by really relaxing your mouth or smiling very slightly. This will take you through a range which will help you to 'hit' your didj's resonant frequency (don't worry, I'm not going to start spouting physics). You could also try varying the pressure between your face and the end of the didj, but don't lose any teeth. Suddenly you will find your lips are really 'buzzing' and the sound will get a lot richer and more vibrant; try and make a mental note of how your lips feel when you hit this and practice it for a while. The drone should now be easier to achieve and you should really concentrate on making it sound as 'bright' as possible whilst learning to let the air out in a controlled way to make it last.

Don't do it for too long at first, just revel in the pride of getting your didj to sound like a didj! If you can't manage it at first, no matter how much you try, don't worry. Just put the didj away, do something else and try again another day – you'll crack it eventually. You might find that, for a few days or weeks, playing the didj for any length of time will make your lips tingle, go numb, or swell up slightly. All these are quite normal and will be very temporary as you adjust to this new skill, if not see a doctor! Joking aside, you might want to take a break if your lips suffer any of these symptoms – I once played too hard for too long and made my lip bleed, not big or clever!

2). Some notes on mouthpieces

If you find you are having real problems you may want to check the size and shape of the mouthpiece. Beeswax on any kind of didj is a good idea as it is easy to shape, comfortable, and has natural anti-bacterial properties. Read the section on creating mouthpieces if your didj doesn't have any wax on it (p.38.). If you think a slight modification is all that is required then try the following: Play the didj for a while so that the wax can warm

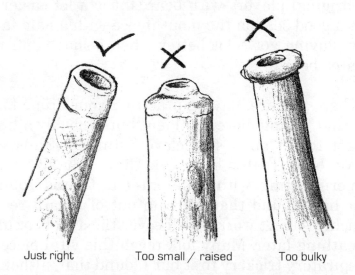

Just right   Too small / raised   Too bulky

Wax on mouthpieces, right and wrong.

up and then mould it with your fingers to either enlarge the hole slightly or bring it in a little at a time. Most players are usually comfortable with a hole somewhere between 3 and 5 centimetres, too small and your lips can't vibrate, too big and you get the same problem with the addition that your breath vanishes very quickly. Although a smaller mouthpiece can help to conserve breath and give you more drone for each breath it may ultimately restrict your ability to do much more than just drone, so try a few sizes until your lips and drone feel really comfortable. I don't wish to labour this stuff too much but these things can really make the difference to the speed with which you progress. It is worth pointing out, at this point, that existence of facial hair can also make a difference to your playing. While it is true that there a lot of Aboriginal players with beards it is a lot easier to get a good seal on the mouthpiece with a bald face, my playing got a lot better when I shaved off my goatee beard!

So here you are, having practised your drone for a bit and feeling more confident but probably a little eager to get on to the 'clever' stuff. Perhaps you have been really keen and have already tried experimenting with different effects and sounds but have found that you run out of breath really quickly – don't worry, we'll cover the art of circular breathing later. Many folk teach this vital piece of respiratory trickery first but I found that, although it is not anywhere near as difficult as it sounds, concentrating on this aspect of playing early on can lead to frustration when wanting to sound like a 'real' didj player from the word go. Right, let's try some fun stuff:

3). Sound variations and rhythm

Playing the basic drone for any length of time sounds nice but there are a great many variants to try. Basically, didj playing is achieving a constant drone whilst embellishing it with all sorts of other wonderful sounds. Whilst managing to do this without pause will require the ability to circular breathe (see p.32) I believe that experimenting with sounds first will make learning more fun. It will also help you to achieve a longer duration of sound without CB, a good skill to have. There are a great many variables involved in determining the sound your didj produces. Putting aside the ones featured in the didj itself I am thinking of the following: the lips and their tightness, the air pressure from the cheeks, lungs or diaphragm, the pressure between the didj and your face, the position of your jaw, teeth and tongue within your mouth and the use of your vocal chords. Each of these can be varied and a massive number of combinations allow almost limitless variations, this is what makes the didjeridoo such a versatile instrument.

Back to the playing: Play your drone sound and really concentrate on making it as rich and full as you can. It is quite likely that your cheeks are only partially inflated or even flat against your teeth, try letting the pressure of the air puff up your cheeks. Drone like this for a while; you might find it takes a while for your cheeks to get fully inflated without this action interfering with your drone sound but when you get it right your drone will become more 'rounded'. Next try varying the pressure from your lungs by squeezing your stomach muscles, either gradually or in a quick huff or puff, so that you your lips buzz faster or slower – listen to what that does to the sound. The drone goes up or down in pitch, an effect you can exaggerate by altering the tightness of your lips – drop your jaw slightly for looser, or smile slightly for tighter. Now try allowing your inflated cheeks to deflate rapidly, even assisting consciously if you can by squeezing them in. This should make a rapid pulse of sound like 'whap' or 'whop'. This effect, and the stomach/lung squeeze, will allow you to add a more percussive element to your playing and you might want to practice doing it in time to some of your favourite music. Don't' worry about further embellishments at this point, just concentrate on the rhythmic 'wooooWhoP woooWhoP' sounds.

The tongue

With your best drone going (nice bright raspy sound) try moving your tongue up to touch the roof of your mouth and slowly sliding it forward until it is nearly touching your teeth. This should produce a satisfying 'wooooEeeeee' sound. Try moving your tongue faster or slower. Another tongue technique is fluttering or trilling (double or triple tonguing if you are a musician). Without the didj try to say 'taka taka taka' and then speed up, or go very fast and vibrate the tongue into a 'tttrrrr' like a spoken French rolled 'r' or even do a purring cat impression. Now try these down the didj ON TOP of your drone, (do not actually use your vocal chords to 'say' the sounds just do the tongue actions), and watch as those around you stare in awe!

You might also try putting your tongue so far forward that you can make a very quick spitting motion, like spitting out a pip, without interrupting the drone – this is a nice punctuation effect. Fluttering your tongue in the main cavity of your mouth, or pushing against your bottom front teeth and letting your tongue arch up to the roof of your mouth, even curling the tip back against the roof of your mouth and then flicking it down. These all produce some great sounds and there are many varieties to try, practice them all until you can manage them without having to try too hard.

The voice

Start droning and then, without altering the drone, start to hum as well. Aim to keep the tongue fairly flat and the throat open so the sound can flow out with the drone. Try humming from a low pitch then slide all the way up to a high one and listen to the wild sounds you can get. Without going into the physics or musical theory of this too heavily, you are passing through the various harmonic frequencies of your didj, some of which are in phase with the drone and some out. What this means is that some frequencies will cause heavy, resonant, vibration like a rattle which will either sound unpleasant or be 'challenging', others will blend with the droned fundamental note to produce a massively rich and vibrant sound. A falsetto scream can be particularly effective.

Next try growling or barking like a dog – 'Gggggrrrrrr, Wuff, Rar!' Let the sound rush out past the drone and try not to bunch up and spring as this will mess up the drone, it should come from your throat. You can even prolong it into a howl 'Aaaoooowwwww'. The idea is to keep the drone the same pitch and speed before, during, and after any additional sounds you throw in.

Other great effects may be achieved by pronouncing vowels, words, phrases or just 'gobbledegook', i.e. nonsensical words. Actually pronounce 'A E I O U' slowly over the drone, making an effort to make them as clear as possible then do it without actually vocalising. Try 'Didjeridoo' in a rhythmic fashion over and over or 'Do-It, Do-It', 'I like didjeridoo', 'A B C D E F..', etc. If you have trouble keeping time when playing or find your sounds just 'wander' and you don't know what to do, just pick a short word or phrase and keep repeating it. It is unlikely anyone will understand what you are actually saying but it will sound like a good rhythmic pattern of sounds.

4). Animals and more besides

Traditional Aboriginal players naturally incorporate the sounds of their environment into their playing as they aim to invoke the link between the real world and the spirit one. Animals found in the Australian Outback feature highly, along with other sounds familiar to them. Here is a list of the non-secret ones that have been shared with non-aboriginals, along with some I've drawn from other sources, and the methods used to recreate them. This list is meant as a 'starter' guide and you will find plenty of other great effects as you experiment for yourself. If you do create a great new sound I'd love to hear about it - drop me a line!

Boomerang: a wing-sectioned, curved, flat of wood used by Aborigines for hunting. When thrown it makes a distinctive whirring noise as it goes away and returns to the thrower. Make this sound by keeping a mid-pitch drone and then rapidly oscillate the tongue forwards and backwards, first at the back of the mouth and then slowly move to the front – 'doooowoowoowooweeweeweeooo' or 'doweeweeweeweewee'.

Cockatoo: Literally say the word over the drone,

start with a mid pitch and end with the 'too' on a higher pitch. As with most vocalisations the lips do not move and the sound should be uttered purely in the throat, this may take some practice to stop it affecting the speed or pitch of the drone.

Cricket; Lower pitched drone, over which can be layered a random pattern of very high-pitched but short trills with the tongue, or even a 'two-tone' trill that mimics 'Cuckoo' in pitch.

Crow: Vocalise the word 'ark' or 'croW' for emphasis. As with all animal calls, try to visualise the animal as you try to imitate it to really bring the sound to life.

Dingo; Drone with a vocalised howl that gets steadily higher pitched and also bark – 'Oooowwwwwwwa' 'wuff' 'ruff-ruff' imitates this wild Australian dog. Also use for a 'standard' dog call.

Gutturals: Not specifically any animal but used to dramatic effect by making a 'gargling' motion with or without a low vocalisation and even adding a low and slow tongue trill.

Kangeroo: Drone with a vocalised 'Do' then a rapid tongue slide, or just say 'DoinG' over and over to simulate the springy step of this Australian marsupial.

Kookaburra: This Australian bird has a raucous, almost mocking, call that has become one of the 'signature' sounds associated with the didj – it is one of the more challenging to recreate. A good stable drone will allow you to introduce an increasingly high pitched vocal and trilled tongue that gives way to a vocalised 'laugh'
– 'oooooooorrrrrrreeeeeeeeAKaKaKaKaKaaaaaa!' and 'Kakow kakoW!.

Snake: a tight, high-pitched, drone with a slow tongue slide and a pronounced inhalation of breath through the nose (see circular breathing), to give the sound of a snake slithering through the undergrowth.

Toots: a toot is a trumpet-like note (a bit like an alpine horn) that is achieved by momentarily tightening the lips right up whilst puffing with a little/lot more pressure. They are hard to master but you might try dropping your jaw slightly or using the 'spitting pip' technique mentioned earlier to get them going. Practice doing them on their own before trying to incorporate them into your playing, where it can be hard to hit them straight from drone and then recover the drone right away. They are used by traditional players to end each 'song' they play as they believe that they must do this to sever their connection with the spirit world, that is created when they are playing, and return to the real world. Once you can manage a good toot you might like to try prolonging it or trying to hit an even higher pitch, some didjs have several toot notes in their harmonic range. To prolong a toot whilst circular breathing is a feat that is difficult to master, and I have heard only very few world-class players make it work successfully. I think of it as a rite of passage into being a really excellent player so it is worth striving for.

Vocalisations; As previously mentioned, you are only limited by your imagination and the range of your voice, so try whatever comes to you. This is your chance to make your own 'signature' sounds.

A note on traditional playing.

If you are interested in playing in a style more akin to traditional Aboriginal players then here are some pointers. The traditional didj player is accompaniment to the songman and dancer and his main role is to provide rhythm so traditional playing tends not to have too many 'western' style rhythm changes or 'wacky' effects. Traditional playing style is best approached on a non-flared didj and one that is not too short. Try to play face on and drop your normal drone pressure until the sound almost starts to break up. What you are aiming for is a low, quite quiet, drone that has a dry sounding 'crackle' to it. When you can achieve this, and it is a lot more difficult than you might think, you can introduce an Aboriginal style rhythm into the drone. Aboriginal language features the vowel sounds Da, Goo, LA so try incorporating them into your playing in a <u>non</u>-vocalised way. Aboriginal playing often follows a cyclic rhythm which can be simple or very complex so try using the vowel sounds in patterns; DaGooLA DaGooLA DaGooLAGooLA or DaGool DAGool (capitals are emphasis). Look out for, and listen to, traditional playing to see how else it differs from more 'Western' styles.

5). Circular Breathing

By this point you will have probably being playing for some weeks or even months, if you have been practising all the various elements covered in the previous sections. You will, of course, have found that your breath runs out after a minute or so and you are in need of that magic something that will allow you to play indefinitely. That magic something is circular breathing and it is seen by many as the single most important part of playing the didj and as some kind of 'trick' or physical impossibility – how to breathe in and out at the same time. The truth of course is that you don't, you use your cheeks to squeeze air out, like the bag on a set of bagpipes, and take a quick sniff of air in through your nose whilst your cheek pressure continues the drone. It really isn't that difficult, it just sounds hard to achieve. I have been told, and have read, many different ways to try to get the hang of CB and everyone will find something that works for them. Here are my suggestions:

Presumably you are, by now, pretty happy with your drone using your lungs as the source. What I want you to do is try using your cheeks instead. Drone normally for 5-10 minutes to warm up then try this: breathe out, off the didj, then use a little air to puff up your cheeks. Now place your lips against the didj and, whilst keeping in mind what your lips and drone normally feel like, use your cheeks to squeeze out the air in them – DO NOT USE YOUR LUNGS AT ALL. You may be disappointed with the farty noise that emerges and it may seem like going all the way back to the beginning again, it isn't. A good trick is to slightly over-tighten your lips as you start to squeeze with the cheeks then let them attain your normal drone tightness as the air starts to spurt out. Keep practising this until you can make a short drone that sounds pretty much like your lung-powered one, do not get disheartened – it took me a lot longer than I bet it will take you.

Once you have got this part right you might try making your squeeze a bit slower and more controlled until you can make your cheek-full of air last as long as possible. If you play off to one side of your mouth you will be at a slight disadvantage as you can only use one inflated cheek effectively, you are running on 50% of air volume. Don't worry about this too much, if you tried playing 'face-on' but couldn't do it you might find that you can manage it once you become more proficient. Playing on one side may even make you more efficient with the available air so that when you are ready to switch to face-on you will find continual droning really easy!

When you are comfortable with your 'squeeze-drone' do it for a couple of minutes then, whilst you squeeze your cheeks, take a quick sniff in with your lungs and hold it whilst you continue squeezing the rest of the air from your cheeks. Hopefully you did it without too much effort. If you didn't manage it first go, try doing it some more or try doing the exercise without the didj, i.e. squeeze out air through tight pursed lips and sniff in at the same time. If you find this difficult then you might try the same kind of exercise with water. Take a largeish sip of water from a glass and hold the water in your mouth, now breathe in and out through your nose. The fact that you can do this without drowning is testament to your ability to 'close-off' the back of your throat so that you can breathe. Now use your cheek muscles to slowly squirt the water from your pursed lips in a steady stream, you might want to do this over, or in, the bath! Whilst you squirt out the water continue to breathe in and out; it is this combination of cheek squeeze and closed off / open throat that constitutes one half of circular breathing so practice a bit. Get this ability sorted out and you are mere moments away from circular breathing so stay with me.

Now, whilst practising your squeeze and sniff routine on the didj (without the water this time!) try letting the air in your lungs, attained with the sniff, back out of your mouth as your squeeze draws to a close. In fact try to exaggerate the motion so that the in-rush of air from your lungs into your cheeks suddenly puffs them back up again as they are becoming empty. You will find that this is probably the true 'tricky' part of the whole venture as you must let your 'closed-off' throat open up again to allow the passage of air from your lungs. If you got this right through sheer effort or it "just happened", no matter – YOU DID IT - you circular breathed! You probably found that the in-rush of air that puffed up your cheeks also produced a wonderful pulse down the didj.

This is the 'real stuff' in terms of percussion, rhythm and timing and is the basis for all traditional Yolngu didj playing. It is as important to your playing too so practice it all you can, in fact if may be a good idea to stop trying all the whizzy animal noises for a while and just practice this vital breathing technique as much as you care to. Once you have got the hang of circular breathing you will find that your playing takes leaps and bounds as you can just let the sounds flow and see where they take you, hopefully somewhere nice.

6). Advanced exercises

After you have been playing for a few months, or

even years, depending on how much time you have been able to invest in practice, <u>you</u> will probably be the best teacher for yourself. You will have a good idea of what works for you with your didj, or didjs, and may not need the next section at all. What follows is mainly a collection of ideas I have picked up along the way that have helped my playing to progress further.

The first suggestions are things that you have already been doing: namely listening to lots of other didj players and playing along with as many other people as you can - be they didj players or other musicians. It is very easy, when learning to play something as absorbing as the didj, to spend too long on the fine details on one's own, instead of diving into playing alongside others. Getting involved with other players is great practice, not only because you can learn from, and encourage, each other but you will feel less inhibited and more likely to try all sorts of crazy ideas. You will also be able to hone your musical skills, like timing and choosing what notes or effects work with different types of music.

Just playing the didj for prolonged periods will strengthen your stomach, cheeks, and chest muscles along with making your diaphragm more effective. However you might want to try some or all of the following:

1). Tense your lips as tight as you can then blow up

you cheeks, now sniff in air through your nose and use it to really puff up your cheeks as though you were playing the didj. Try moving the air around with your cheek muscles so it bulges out different bits of your face and really stretches them out, but be careful not to strain yourself. This is great for building your cheek muscles but makes sure they also have flexibility to contain a lot of air.

NOTE: If you feel dizzy or get a headache when doing this, or any other of the exercises STOP.
You might also want to save these exercises for when you are alone in case you alarm anyone. I tend to do stuff like this whilst I am driving long-distance on unchallenging roads. It is funny if anyone catches sight of you trying these exercises, they can be great for getting seats on buses and trains too!

2). Try the first exercise again only this time allow the air to escape very slowly from your lips as you attain the furthest cheek stretch you feel comfortable with. As the air forces its way out, start circular breathing to refill your lungs and prolong the whole process. Do not do this for too long as it puts your whole respiratory system under strain. It is great for building strength within your circular breathing technique.

3). Make a fist with either hand and press the thumb side of your hand against your mouth like you were about to play a didj. Now blow out hard so that the air escapes through the gaps in your fingers, then as the air runs out try to suck air back in again - there will be a lot of resistance! Vary the resistance either way by slightly opening your fist so that you don't end up seeing stars! This exercise should not be used too often or for too long but it is an excellent way to strengthen your stomach and chest muscles and build your diaphragm for really powerful playing.

4). Take a length of clean plastic or rubber hose, say 40cms long, and bend it into a U shape. Place one end into your mouth (that's why it needs to be clean!) and blow gently to create a stream of air that exits vertically from the other end of the up-turned pipe. Whilst doing this get a friend(!) to gently place a Ping-Pong ball in the stream of air where it should balance and bob up-and-down. This is like the child's toy that does something similar with a plastic 'smokers' pipe, in fact if you can get one of these even better! This might seem completely crazy, but with the ball balanced on the air stream, start to circular breath. The ball will bob up-and-down violently and may even fall off, this is a great exercise for making sure your circular breath transitions are nice and smooth!

5). Unless you were already a musician or have natural talent in this regard you might want to practice your timing and ability to maintain a rhythm. The best way to practice this is to play with other musicians but failing that you might consider buying a digital metronome. They can be purchased in musical instrument stores for under £30 and can produce a wide range of beats to play along to. Even some professional musicians use a similar device, to feed them a timing 'tick' through a discreet ear-piece whilst playing or singing.

6). The last exercise I'm going to suggest is no ground-breaker. It is practice and lots more practice. It seems obvious but I know from experience that it is always tempting, once one has learned a certain repertoire, to stay within the confines of what you know when playing. Always be willing to push things a bit further than you really want to go and don't be afraid to make mistakes, even when playing publicly. If there is something you don't like doing because it is hard or you are not good at it then do it a lot. This is the story with me and my attempts at prolonged toots.

Making or modifying a mouthpiece

Most didjs will require the addition of a beeswax mouthpiece to allow them to be played comfortably. If your didj has a non-waxed mouthpiece that you are happy with then you may want to just sand it smooth and varnish it. As long as it is comfortable to play and provides an adequate seal to your face then this may be better, as even beeswax may interfere with the drone at a very minimal level. Beeswax may be bought from a craft or candle-maker's suppliers, and may be in 'ingot' or pellet form. If you need to modify an existing mouthpiece just follow the instructions but add to what you already have. There are two ways to produce a mouthpiece: with moulded or molten wax.

The moulded method (A)

Place the wax in a plastic bag and place it in your pocket or against your body. Do something else for 5-10 minutes, like play your didj! Take the now warmed wax and roll it out onto a flat surface with the palm of your hand until you get a long sausage shape. Take this and press one end of the sausage horizontally onto the playing end of the didj. Mould the sausage down onto the didj with your thumb and move round the didj until you meet the starting point (see p.40). Pinch off any excess length and mould your new mouthpiece until it fits you well, pushing your finger into the hole and easing back the edge to make it larger or pushing down and in towards the hole to make it smaller. Finish it off so that the hole is reasonably round and the surface of the wax is quite flat, and avoid leaving a bulk of wax that stops your face pressing against the end of the didj. This method is good if you need to reduce a very large sized bore.

The molten method (B)

This is a bit more difficult but can lead to a superior result. Take an old glass coffee jar or similar receptacle, making sure that it is wider than the playing end of your didj, and break up the wax into the jar. Stand the jar in an old saucepan with an inch or two of water in it. Put the whole lot on a stove and heat until the water boils then gently stir the wax as it starts to melt. Aim to get about 5cms depth of molten wax in the bottom of the jar. Take the jar out (careful it will be hot!) and stand it on the floor, which you have protected with old newspaper. Turn your didj upside down and carefully dip the playing end into the molten wax at the bottom of the jar (B below). Lift the didj out of the wax and let the drips fall back into the jar. Allow this layer of wax to cool for a second or two and repeat this action.

Your goal is to build up several coats of wax. Keep checking that the internal diameter of your didj mouthpiece is not becoming too small. Once it looks about right leave the wax on the didj to dry for ten minutes or so then try playing it. You may need to

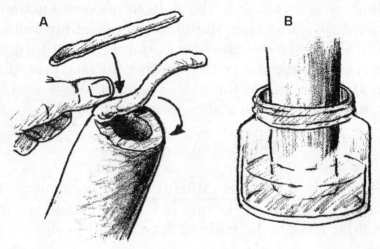

A   B

smooth off any lumps left by the dripping wax and to make small adjustments until it allows you to play your best sound. A beeswax mouthpiece should last almost indefinitely, especially if you keep a clean plastic bag over it when the didj is not in use or it is in a didj bag. The most care the mouthpiece may need will be the odd wipe-over with your thumb if it gets 'hairy' or dirty and an occasional re-tune if its shape starts to wander. If it gets really messy you may want to strip it off and put a fresh one on or just add a new layer of clean wax over the old.

Making a didjeridoo

I think you will agree with me that playing the didj is very satisfying. To make your own didj and then play it can be even more so. Basic didj construction doesn't require any particularly specialist tools unless you have set your sights on hollowed-out wooden didjs (more on these later). You should get by with a saw, a measuring tape, pencil, file and/or sandpaper, and some beeswax. If you want to make didjs in certain musical keys you might want to purchase a digital instrument tuner to tune your didj into pitch. These can be purchased for £15 to £30 from musical instrument stores and will give you a simple display of whatever note is played near the tuner, including sharps and flats.

The construction of plastic, metal, or even cardboard didjs is no more complicated than selecting a pipe of the right diameter (see notes in earlier section on types of didjs) and cutting it to your desired length - shorter for higher pitch, longer for lower pitch. Here is a rough guide to lengths when using typical PVC water pipe with a 3.5cm bore: Length in centimetres / pitch. 130/C. 115/D. 105/E. 98/F. All you need do to make a cut pipe ready for playing is file the rough ends and add a wax mouthpiece, (see pages 38-40).

As pipe like this is so cheap you might even try making a didj for each of the major musical notes and try playing them in turn. You will find that each note has characteristics that you can incorporate into your playing, and will allow you to see which note you tend to prefer before buying a Eucalyptus didj in the same key. You can even try making a slide didj by finding sections of pipe that fit closely into one another, but in practice this can be pretty tricky.

Making wooden didjs is a whole different ball-game and does need some wood-working skill and some specialist tools. The only method that I would suggest you try is the split-wood technique. As mentioned previously, the basics of this are to cut an appropriate length of wood in half, hollow out the two sections and glue back together. To do this with any success you should try to use seasoned wood and not 'green' wood that is freshly cut. A good source of wood is a timber yard, who may carry fencing poles made from chestnut and other woods. These poles are the right kind of length and girth, though they can be a little on the thin size for a really good sized didj. It is quite likely that the timber yard can cut the pole clean in half along its length for a reasonable fee – saving you a lot of hard work. Take the sections home and mark up guidelines for a channel running down the centre

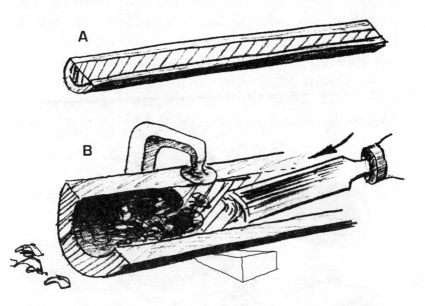

A

B

of each of the halves (A). You should allow the channel to flare out from around 3cm at one end to as wide as you can at the other end, bearing in mind that the wall must be at least 1cm thick in all places. Secure one half at a time to a sturdy table or wood-working bench with G clamps with the cut surface of the poles facing upwards. Take a large and sharp (so be careful!) wood gouge and start to remove the central section of wood between your marked-out lines (B). This may take a long time and will be hard work. You can speed this work up by utilising a drill with a large borer bit but you will need to be very careful as these are sharp and it is easy to do damage to the didj or to yourself.

Once you have hollowed out each side, up to your scribed lines try holding the two halves back together and check for a good fit. It will be important to gouge the cut sections as soon as possible after the pole has been cut in half, and avoid damp environments or your sections may warp and prove difficult to join back together. Assemble as many G clamps and belts or straps as

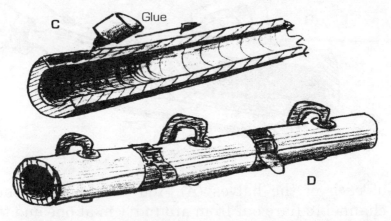

you can, these will need to fit comfortably around the two sections. Using a specialist wood glue, join the two sections together following the adhesive instructions carefully (C). After checking that the two halves match correctly along the full length of the pole, bind the two halves together very tightly using the clamps and belts all along the length at regular intervals. Lay the pole somewhere cool and dry to allow the glue to set, and allow more drying time than the glue recommends. Check the pole after the glue has cured and fill any gaps you can see with wood filler, then remove the clamps. Allow the didj to stand for few days to stabilise before playing, even though you will be eager to try it!

If you have set your heart on making a didj that flares out toward the non-playing end then you are setting yourself a real task! Use seasoned, wind-fallen, wood if at all possible and follow the instructions above with the following additions.

Strip all the bark off the section of timber and get it cut in half on an electric bandsaw, this may be tricky for even a wood-yard so expect to pay for the privilege. Mark up the interior of the wood as before but this time you need to mark up the outside edge of what will be the top end of the didj as well, it will need to taper in to about 6-8cm width. Make some saw cuts that come in at 90° from the edges of the wood and stop just short of the line that will become the outside of the didj. Do this every 5cms, on each side, and on each piece of wood, until the point where the scribed line you marked reaches the existing outside edges on the pieces of timber. Hollow and join the didj halves as before. The saw marks will act as depth guides to allow you cut away the thickness of the top of the didj with a saw. Do not go to the full depth of the saw marks, just roughly cut away and shape the playing end of the didj to make it thinner. Finish the shape of the taper off with a spoke shave or a plane until you have just removed these saw cuts, that way you will be left with an outer wall of at least 1cm thick. This tolerance is why this type is so tricky! Sand and varnish the outside of your didj to seal it, or paint it if you wish. You should be justifiably proud of your achievement.

Hopefully your finished didj, of whatever type, should play just as well as any other manufactured didj with the added bonus that you made it yourself pretty inexpensively. All it needs to finish it off is a good beeswax mouthpiece, but feel free to leave it un-waxed if you get a good, comfortable, seal when playing it.

Making a didj bag

If you have access to a sewing machine, or a willing friend, you might like to make a didj bag to carry your didj(s) around in. Choose any reasonably thick and strong cloth, denim and canvas are good materials to use. Measure your didj and note the length and girth of the thickest section, usually the non-playing end. Add 30cms to the length measurement and double the girth measurement and add 15cms – this will give you the width and length of the sheet of fabric you will need (A). Mark out the dimensions on the flat sheet with chalk and cut out with sharp scissors (you might ask an adult to do this – just kidding!). Lay the cut sheet flat

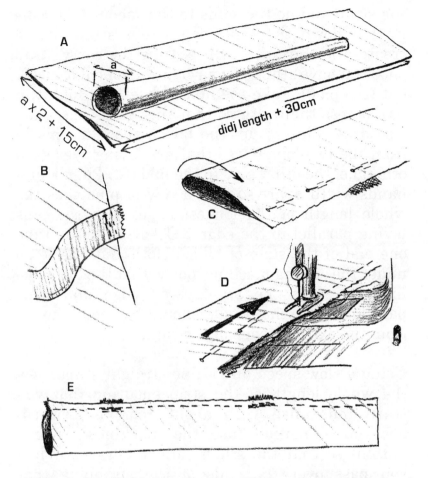

A

a

a x 2 + 15cm

didj length + 30cm

B

C

D

E

with the 'outside' upwards. Next take a length of webbing strap (looks like a car seatbelt and is bought from specialist shops, or use any strong strap of material about 2-3cms wide, and cut to about 80cms long. Measure 70cms down the long edge of your fabric and put the end of the strap so that it is just over the edge and running 90° to it and pin it in place (B). Then take the other end of the strap and do the same to that about 50-60cms further down the same edge. Your strap should create a low arc that will become the carry strap once you have stitched your bag and folded it inside out (see p.50). Take the fabric sheet and fold it in half across the width so that the 'inside' faces up. Use dress pins to pin the fabric about 2.5cms in from the two long edges that are laying over each other, i.e. the other side to the fold (C). Pin about a hands-width apart so that a row of pins goes the whole length of the longest edge, with the pins laying parallel to the edge NOT at 90° to it. Take one end of the strip of folded cloth and line it up under the sewing machine foot so that the foot edge lines up with the two-layered edge and runs parallel to it – the needle should be about 1cm in from the extreme edge of the cloth (D).

Using a slow speed and a fine straight stitch, sew the whole length of the strip ensuring that you start and finish with about 1cm of 'forward-backwards' motion (use the machine's reverse button) so that the stitch cannot unravel. When you pass over the ends of the strapping that protrude from the edge slow down, and do a few back-and-forths to ensure a strong join. Cut off the thread to separate the sewn length of cloth from the machine and check your handiwork (E).

Next measure across the width of the sewn tube of fabric and create a circle about two-thirds as wide as your measurement. Use a compass to mark out this circle on the cloth, or find something the right diameter like a tin lid (F). Cut this out and pin it so that it sits in the end of the sewn fabric 'tube', furthest away from the strapping end. This is quite tricky and you may find you need to trim the circle down to make it fit but you should finish up with the end looking like the bottom of a round bag (G). Stitch this just in from the edge as before, stopping to re-adjust the length of cloth as you go – it will bunch up awkwardly as you sew.

Pull out all the pins carefully, check the whole length of cloth, which should look like (H). Put your arm down inside the bag and turn it inside out. You should have a bag sealed at one end with your strap protruding from the sewn seam to produce a carry strap – congratulations your didj has a bag. All you need to do to finish off is sew a 40cm length of ribbon or bootlace onto the outside of the bag (I),

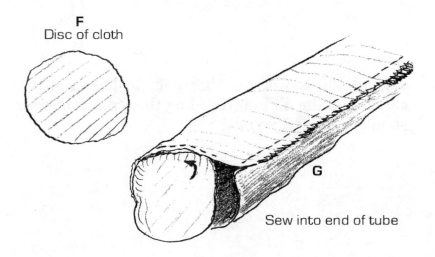

F
Disc of cloth

G

Sew into end of tube

about 25cm down from the open end. Sew the centre of the length of lace onto the bag so that, after you slide your didj into the bag, you can fold over the excess length of the bag. Use the lace to tie

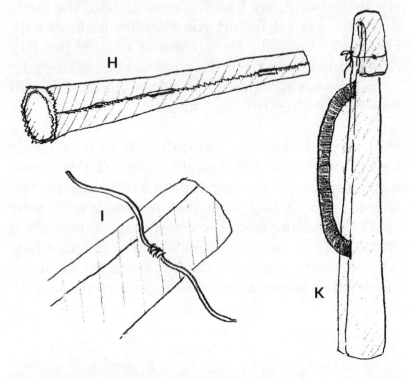

around the top of the didj bag, to hold the bag closed and the didj in (K). Sling the strap over your shoulder and off you go!

Further references

Charities
Tasca Trust. Helping Aboriginal communities.
Tel: Joy Rainey on 01386 47471

Didjeridoo / aboriginal instrument importers
Aboriginalia – Tel: 01386 853770
Australia Shop - Tel: 020 7836 2292
Australian Cultural Exp. – Tel: 020 8902 0832
Siesta – Tel: 01227 786066

Didjeridoo makers (usually split wood)
Antic Earthworks – Tel: 01363 881108
Knock on Wood – Tel: 0113 242 9146
Sacred Elder - Tel: 01203 581835

Books (small selection)
Dreamings: The Art of Aboriginal Australia, Edited by Peter Sutton.
Aboriginal Art, Wally Caruna.
Voices of the First Day, Robert Lawlor.
Understanding Aboriginal Culture, C. Havecker.
Aboriginal Mythology, M. Nyoongah.
A Secret Country, J. Pilger.

Recording Artists and bands
Look out for CDs, Tapes and performances from these great players, sorry to all those who didn't get a mention - drop me your details for next time. Ankala. Axis. Mark Atkins. Alastair Black. David Blonski. David Blanasi. Stephen Cragg. Cyrung.

Alan Dargin. Didjworks. Dr. Didg. Ed Dury. Shaun Farrenden. Ganga Giri. Goma. David Hudson. Phillip Jackson. Stephen Kent. Charlie McMahon. Nomad. Outback. Phillip Peris. Steve Roach. Stephen Robson. Sacred Elder. Shining Bear. Shozo. Tribal Drift. Richard Walley. Yomyano. Yothu Yindi. (& me!).

Didj listings on the Internet.
Like it or not this modern technology is rapidly transforming access to information. Although the speed at which things change on the 'net means that addresses (or URLs) can become out-of-date very quickly I thought I'd list some of the more interesting sites that have been around for a while. Type address as you see it into your browser address window and hit the return key.

http://www.didjeridu-uk.org Homesite of Didjeridu UK, lots of useful listings for didj players in the UK.

http://nav.webring.yahoo.com/hub?ring=didg ring&list Main index for a Web Ring, lots of sites all linked together.

http://www.mills.edu/LIFE/CCM/DIDJERIDU/ Home of the Dreamtime didj server with alot of information and didj links. Check out the player listing for a huge database of names of didj players world-wide.

http://partners.mamma.com/HotSheet?lang=1 &timeout=4&query=Didgeridoo&qtype=0
Index from a search on 'Didgeridoo' on Hotsheet. Lots to check out, you might also run searches on the various spellings of didjeridoo, didgeridu, etc.

http://www.aboriginalart.com.au/ Home site with links in several languages. Loads of Aboriginal cultural information, art, didjs, etc.

http://www.rdrop.com/~mulara/links/making. html Index page for a huge amount of info on making didjs of all kinds along with other useful stuff for recording, playing, etc.

http://www.candlemakers.co.uk/cmproduct/c msframe.html Mail order source of good quality beeswax, get together with some friends for a bulk purchase discount!

Supplies
Beeswax: Candle Makers Supplies.
Tel 02076024031.or see net link above.

Plastic pipes, tools: B&Q, Payless DIY, Sainsburys Homebase (all UK). Also try Golfing shops for plastic sleeves which fit together for an instant basic slide didj.

Timber: Timberyards, check your local telephone directory.

About the author

I am English but that doesn't stop me being massively interested in all things that make 'funny noises'. The didjeridoo happens to be the most sophisticated of these 'things' and makes a very nice noise indeed. Although I never trained to be a musician I have had a very keen interest in, and a strong desire to create, music for most of my life, a desire that is being satisfied as I move along with the didj. In addition to the didj, I also harbour a passion for over-tone or harmonic singing; the deliberate exaggeration of the harmonics created when singing a fundamental note. If you want to know more try an Internet search for the words 'overtone singing', or drop me a line.

I am largely self-taught when it comes to playing the didjeridoo so my suggestions come mainly from personal experience. However, I cannot claim to be completely without assistance and I would like to send a very big 'thank you' to the following people who have helped me understand and get to grips with this great instrument. Derek Furlong for early tuition and repeated encouragement, Shining Bear and Kyle for broadening my knowledge, Laurence and Adam of www.didjeridu-uk.org for putting together the annual DidjFest event, and to all those who have spent time sharing their words, or playing, with me. Other thanks must also go to my parents for buying me my first didj and for tolerating all my odd hobbies over the years, Steve

Lawson and Sebastian Merrick for words of encouragement, Geof Thompson for 'beta testing' and finally, to Rosie - from the heart, for editorial and putting up with me!

I hope you have enjoyed this book and have been inspired to continue to play didj. If you would like more information on learning to play, or feel you would benefit from tutored lessons, please contact me at   . I am also currently running regular (monthly) gatherings for didj players in London, so contact me for details.

If you feel inclined to write a letter of solidarity, in support of Aboriginal claims to Land Rights address it to:

Minister for Aboriginal Affairs
Senator John Herron
Parliament House
Canberra ACT 2600
Australia